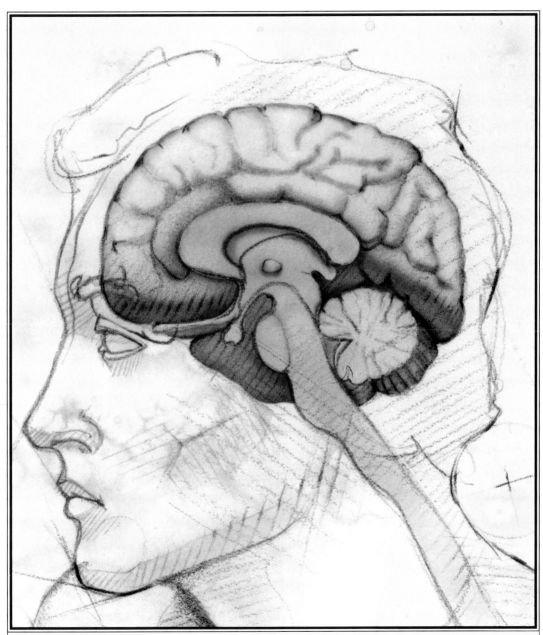

The brain is the control center of the human body

THE *Brain*

Anne Fitzpatrick

A⁺
Smart Apple Media

COPYRIGHT

Published by Smart Apple Media

1980 Lookout Drive, North Mankato, MN 56003

Designed by Rita Marshall

Copyright © 2004 Smart Apple Media. International copyright reserved in all countries. No part of this book may be reproduced in any form without written permission from the publisher.

Printed in the United States of America

Pictures by Bonnie Hofkin, The Image Finders (Michael Philip Manheim), Diane Meyer, Tom Myers, Photo Researchers/Science Source (David M. Phillips), Bonnie Sue Rauch, Tom Stack & Associates (W. Perry Conway), Unicorn Stock Photos (Joel Dexter, W. B. Hoffmann)

Library of Congress Cataloging-in-Publication Data

Fitzpatrick, Anne, 1978- The brain / by Anne Fitzpatrick.

p. cm. — (The human body) Includes bibliographical references and index.

Summary: Introduces the human brain, its parts, how it works, and what it helps us accomplish. Includes an activity to determine which side of the brain is more used by the reader.

ISBN 1-58340-310-8

1. Brain—Juvenile literature. [1. Brain.] I. Title. II. Human body systems (Mankato, Minn.).

QP376 .F53 2003   612.8'2—dc21   2002030624

First Edition 9 8 7 6 5 4 3 2 1

THE *Brain*

CONTENTS

The Driver's Seat

Imagine that the human body is a spaceship. Where would the pilot be? In the brain! The brain is the body's driver's seat. All of the information gathered by the eyes, ears, nose, mouth, and sense of touch is sent to the brain. Every movement that the body makes starts with a message from the brain.

The brain is also the spaceship's library. It is the place where memories are kept. A memory of a fun day at the zoo and a memory about tomorrow's homework assignment would both

Your brain tells you what you see, smell, and feel

be stored in the brain. The brain keeps all of the information that the senses receive. Suppose the eyes see an apple. The brain stores a picture of the apple. The next time the eyes see an apple, the brain will compare it to all the pictures in its memory. When it matches the apple the eyes see to the apple picture in its memory, the brain knows what it is seeing.

By the time a person gets to be five years old, his or her brain has nearly reached its full, adult size.

The brain remembers what an apple looks like

Your brain keeps a record of everything you see

Mapping the Brain

There are three major parts of the brain. The **cerebrum** is the biggest part. It receives information from the senses, stores memories, and does all the thinking and learning. The cerebrum also controls voluntary movements. Voluntary movements are movements that a person must think about, such as running or moving a hand. ➤ Involuntary movements, such as breathing, blinking, and the beating of the heart, are controlled by the brain stem. A person does not

The brain sends messages at speeds of about 290 miles (465 km) per hour.

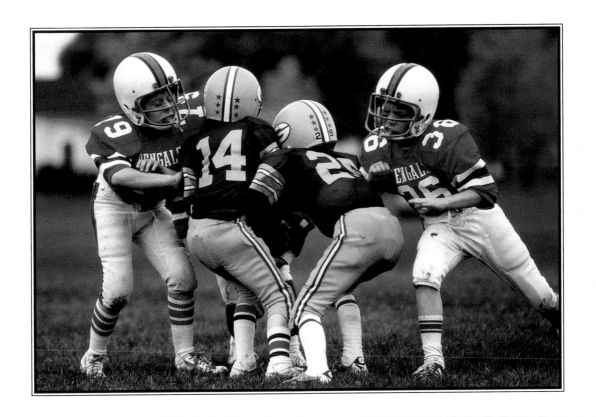

have to think about involuntary movements. The brain makes

them happen automatically. The brain stem is the part of the

brain that looks like a little tail. The **cerebellum** is the

The cerebrum allows us to think and move around

small lump at the back of the brain. It **coordinates** everything the body does. Information from the senses must be matched up with messages sent to the muscles. When the eyes see a ball coming toward them, they send a message to the cerebellum about where the ball is, how fast it is moving, and how big it is. The cerebellum uses the information to tell the hand how to catch the ball.

Brain Messengers

The brain is made of **cells** called **neurons**. Long strings of neurons also stretch throughout the body to carry messages

to and from the brain. Each neuron can send (and receive)

messages to more than 1,000 other neurons. ◣ Neurons

create pathways when they send a message over and over

The cerebellum gives us the coordination to play sports

again. These pathways are like trampled snow on a sidewalk in the winter. After a person has walked on the sidewalk over and over again, a path forms and it is easier to walk. Neurons can send messages faster and more easily along the pathways they create. That is why tasks such as tying a shoe or reciting multiplication tables become easier the more they are done.

If all of a body's neurons were laid end to end, they would be about 2,500 miles (4,000 km) long!

This is an up-close look at the neurons in a brain

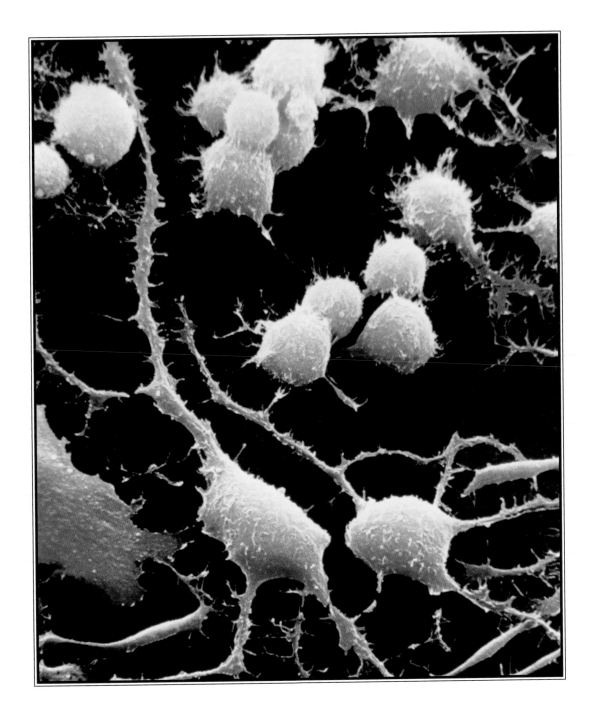

Brain Health

At birth, a person already has all the neurons he or she will ever have. Neurons cannot be replaced when they die.

There are fewer and fewer neurons as a person ages. This is why it gets harder to remember things as a person gets older. ➤ The skull is the hardest bone in the body. It protects the

A normal, healthy brain is made up of more than 10 billion neurons.

fragile brain. Inside the skull, the brain floats around in fluid.

The fluid keeps the brain from banging against the inside of the skull. But even with this protection, the brain can be easi-

ly hurt. A hard bump on the head can cause some neurons to

die. It is a good idea to wear a helmet when riding a bike,

rollerblading, skateboarding, or playing hockey.　　It is

A helmet protects the skull and brain from injury

important to keep the body healthy so it can take care of the brain. Healthy foods provide the brain with the nutrients it needs, and exercise helps the body send oxygen to the brain.

The brain can get exercise, too. The more **A full-grown brain weighs** a person thinks and learns, the smarter, **about three pounds (1.4 kg),** stronger, and faster the brain gets. **or as much as a carton of** Reading a book is a great brain workout! **orange juice.**

Reading and playing make a brain smart and strong

Right Brain, Left Brain

The right side of the body is controlled by the left side of the brain, and the left side of the body is controlled by the right side of the brain. Most people use one side more than the other. Try the following activity to see which side you use.

What You Do

1. Pick an object across the room. Hold a finger out so that it blocks the object from your sight. Now close your right eye. Open it and close your left eye. Which eye could not see the object?
2. Find some stairs to walk up or down. Which foot did you use to step on the first stair?
3. Write your name. Which hand did you use, your right or your left?

Some scientists think the left side of the brain is used more for things like math, and the right side for things like painting a picture.

The right side of your brain helps you paint and draw

INFORMATION

Index

Words to Know

brain stem (BRANE stem)—the lower part of the brain; it controls automatic movements

cells (SELLZ)—the tiny building blocks that make up all living things

cerebellum (SARE-uh-BEH-lum)—the part of the brain under the cerebrum; it coordinates the muscles' movements

cerebrum (suh-REE-brum)—the main part of the brain; it controls voluntary movements and thoughts

coordinates (koh-OR-deh-nayts)—causes to work well together

neurons (NOO-ronz)—the kind of cells that make up the brain and its messengers

Read More

Angliss, Sarah. *The Controls: Brain and Nervous System.* Thameside Press, 1999.

Cromwell, Sharon. *Why Do I Laugh or Cry? And Other Questions About the Nervous System.* Des Plaines, Ill.: Rigby Interactive Library, 1998.

Llamas, Andreu. *The Nervous System.* Milwaukee: Gareth Stevens Publishing, 1998.

Internet Sites

Brain Pop Health: Nervous System
http://www.brainpop.com/health/
nervous

Neuroscience for Kids
http://faculty.washington.edu/chudler/
neurok.html

Mammalian Brain Collections
http://www.brainmuseum.org